Homecoming 4

Winter Solstice 2024

Nature

Aurochs Underground Press

Aurochs: Homecoming 4: Nature

ISBN 978-1-7396972-7-3

Published by Aurochs Underground Press, Bath, UK

HOMECOMING

A JOURNAL OF NEW ANIMIST WRITING

Edited by Jack Wolf

List of Artworks

COVER ART & FINAL PAGE:

Hannah Willow : Owl

INTERIOR :

Carrie Osborne:

Ty Canol: 4, 29, 44, 64

Ink Tree: 13

Raven: 23

Red Kite: 35

Roots: 16, 31, 39, 54, 62

Contents

JONATHAN WOOLLEY

Animism and Nature

There is a quiet revolution taking place in the Western world's relationship with nature. As the environmental crisis worsens, and the necessary political and economic transformation fails to materialise, there is a turning to more radical solutions. Whether this involves calling for legal rights for ecosystems, or shifts in the language used in prayer, prose and poetry, people from the Western world are beginning to recognise personhood beyond the human realm. Earlier this year, Paul Powesland, a barrister, was called to jury service, and he asked to swear his oath on a vial of water from the river Roding. Paul tends the river lovingly, planting trees along its banks, removing rubbish from its waters, even founding a charity to protect it. When quizzed by the judge on his request, Paul "told him the river was effectively my god, and that I hold the river to be sacred". Such an act runs contrary to the prevailing position in England - and most of the Western world - that nature is a mere series of physical systems, governed by the insensible operation of impersonal laws. As Philippe Descola famously explored, in Western culture, the mechanical domain of Nature is kept carefully separate from the interpersonal world of human culture. Under such a regime, rivers cannot be gods.

While it may be radical for a white Western Oxbridge-educated barrister to say such things, these ideas are nothing new. From the Yukaghir to the Anishinaabe, from the Gamilaroi to the !Kung, from the Bedouin to the Japanese, people the world over - particularly indigenous peoples - experience our cosmos as a living, enchanted domain, brimming with other-than-human inhabitants. In numerous cases, such experiences undergird a deep-seated ethos of care and respect for the living world, far beyond anything Western environmentalism has been able to sustain. But for much of the Modern Age, animism was dismissed as superstition - and the fact that the West was interpreting the cosmos in mechanistic ways was viewed as evidence of its unique civilisational superiority. But as Joshua Schrei argues, the fact that the mechanistic cosmos of the West is so unusual could also indicate that animism is actually the normative position - the normal way for human beings to experience the world around them. If this is the case, then the Western, naturalist era represents not an intellectual triumph, but a tragic, collective error - a denial of a crucial part of our common human nature.

Readers of this volume will no doubt be aware that in Britain - and in much of the Western World - animism, new or otherwise, is not merely disbelieved, but is a target of disdain. Although this represents a considerable improvement from the outright persecution that took place in previous centuries, this dismissive attitude shows how liberal tolerance is often provisional. It is far more acceptable to believe in the existence of a creator god who transcends nature, than to embrace the presence of spirits who dwell within it. During my own ethnographic fieldwork with land managers in the English countryside, I found it interesting to note how any momentary lapse into talking about nature in social terms - ascribing agency to a blackcap defending his nest, or seeing something transcendently beautiful in a butterfly - would often be followed by a verbal disavowal of "anthropomorphism" by the individual concerned. While attitudes are changing, the sincere acceptance of genuine relationships with nature - that acknowledge personhood in our surroundings - provokes incredulity, strenuous distancing, and mockery, in a way other spiritual beliefs and practices do not.

The fact that animism and "anthropomorphism" are actively mocked and dismissed as "weird" is itself revealing. All human societies have developed powerful socio-psychological features for protecting their members from breaches in conduct that undermine the cultural fabric: taboos. Taboos place strict prohibitions on certain substances, words, and behaviours, leading those things to provoke disgust in the people exposed to them. Mary Douglas highlights the way in which taboos are created around things that don't fit established categories - what she famously dubbed "matter out of place". Bodily fluids, for example, transgress the category of inside and outside the body, and therefore they are frequently seen as offensive or disgusting. Relating to nature, I suggest, seems to provoke a very similar kind of reaction, because it breaches the categorical Western distinction between human and non-human worlds.

Various strategies are deployed to diffuse breaches of taboos, and soothe this sense of disgust - such as othering and humour. While we may have rejected the explicit racist evolutionism of Edward Tylor that cast animism at the bottom of a hierarchical process of advancement that culminated in (Tylor's own) scientific atheism, Westerners still assure themselves that animism is a decidedly non-Western phenomenon - a feature of exotic cultures far away, a safe distance from our own way of life. When, against all expectations, animism is displayed by Western people, it is ridiculed and dismissed as a foolish eccentricity. Eminent French sociologist Bruno Latour is typical of scholars who act in this way, having written dismissively of those who anthropomorphise Gaia as a goddess, without actually citing any of their writings, or describing them ethnographically. Even the new Nature Writing is full of careful hedging - enthusing about the emotional and intellectual heft of the living world, before hurrying to distance itself from the supposedly superstitious idea that natural things might, at times, be persons. Out of print, people mince their words even less. I was once referred to by a fellow anthropologist as "That weirdo who told Marilyn Strathern he was a Druid".

This anti-animist chauvinism highlights how important the nature-culture divide is to Western civilisation. Its importance can be seen most sharply within our philosophy of property. Private property in the Western world is directly inspired by Roman Law, which awarded vast powers to the owners of property - the right to control, exploit, even destroy their possessions. Through the institutions of slavery and the Roman family, this dominion extended over human lives, as both slaves and children were seen as the property of the *pater familias*. Since then, the tide of what (and who) is considered property has ebbed and flowed, and the notion of personhood has followed it. The historical anthropologist Jane Schneider describes how the erasure of personhood from animals, plants, and landscapes, converts what once were manifestations of gods or abodes of spirits into inert resources that could be exploited by urban elites. Schneider's account highlights how the intimacy between rural people and the landscapes in which they live often give rise to animistic relations that override strict boundaries between nature and society. Seeing nature in this way makes extraction for profit more difficult. If a forest is holy, freighted with relationships, meaning and memory, it becomes harder to justify chopping it down. And so urban elites - who benefitted from extractivism - condemned animism as heresy, with relations with other-than-humans being increasingly circumscribed with the passing of time. Given the central importance of extractivism to Western political economy today, it isn't hard to see how profoundly destabilising animism could be. I argue that this provides a far more powerful explanation of why animism is so strenuously rejected in Western countries, than any effort to link it to specific religious or philosophical developments, like the Enlightenment or the rise of Christianity. This explanation also avoids the unfortunate and factually incorrect implication that indigenous peoples are less rigorous, less analytical, or less rational than the West.

Recognising the challenge animism poses to property rights, even helps us prise apart variations within the Western world. The English and the Americans place the right to private property in particularly high regard, as de Toqueville once noted, so it stands to reason that they should oppose animistic relationships with particular ferocity. While the Italians may still embrace their saints, and the Icelanders may still build roads around the homes of the hidden folk, the Anglophone world has chosen wherever possible to exorcize its animating spirits. Because animism acts as a solvent that breaks down the fundamental barricade in the Western universe - between nature, which can be owned, and persons, who own it - that makes modern capitalist societies possible. As Schneider argues, the persecution and forced conversion of animists in Europe and elsewhere was a kind of psychological warfare to make extractivism possible. And in the heart of possessive individualism - namely, English-speaking nations - we find that puritanical exertions are most intense.

All these exertions to police the distinction between humankind and the rest of nature evaporate in light of one clear fact: humans are part of nature too. If nature is merely an impersonal lattice of physical cause and effect that can only be properly described in scientific terms, then so are we. We have found no unique, secret, biophysical ingredient that makes humankind especially deserving of the animating touch of personhood; indeed, recent discoveries in neuroscience suggest that free will itself may be, from a scientific point of view, an illusion. So if the concept of society and the persons that inhabit it are permitted to have any reality at all - and it must - then it should in principle extend beyond the narrow confines of our species. While there are people who believe humanity are mere robots acting out biochemical algorithms, I sincerely doubt that this is fully and constantly how they experience the world, and the only means by which they interpret the behaviour of those around them. Indeed, those who come close, are often the worst amongst us. Because if even human beings are just biological machines, why bother relating to them - respecting them, caring for them, empathising with them - either?

This is the final, sociopathic, solipsistic twist to possessive individualism. If you create an absolute divide between things that can be owned, and those who own them - then it is easy to banish people from one category into the other. If you make it so owners have an absolute right to treat their possessions however they see fit, and make this constitutive of their very identity, then it becomes ever harder to advocate on behalf of those who are owned. Slavery, colonialism, bondage, and patriarchy were all vastly empowered by an intellectual framework that marked out spaces where relationality was eclipsed by dominion; spaces that could be inhabited by people who didn't count, because they weren't really people anyway. The erasure of animism was part of a long, protracted and bitter process of de-sensitising whole societies to the instrumental treatment of a sacred, living world - and it should not surprise us that many hundreds of millions of human beings could be on the receiving end of such mistreatment, if the interests of the propertied were served by it. Teaching people how to ignore potential relationships takes considerable effort; we are naturally an empathetic animal. So people are told to practice on rivers and mountains, before turning what they have learned on their fellow human beings. If you can't potentially see personhood in everyone, then it can potentially be stripped from *anyone*. You, too, could be made into property.

This may seem far fetched, but the rapacious appetites of a political economy based on possessive individual are already touching most of us. As Jaron Lanier observed, Facebook and other social media platforms have essentially privatized friendship, transforming our deepest relationships, interests, conversations, and creations into shallow commodities that can be sold to data brokers, advertisers and political parties. These applications are designed to devour our attention, so that we have less and less available for relations that take place elsewhere and are thus resistant to digital commodification.

By pointing out a simple fact - that humans have the power to relate to everything, and that in this are truths, rather than ignorance - animism can inoculate our culture against the relentless, devouring tendency towards turning people into property, by dissolving the rationalisations that make this possible. It calls us back into a kind of immanent relatedness to all life that makes commodification and extractivism extremely difficult. It is for this reason that Western culture cannot tolerate animism, relying on humour and othering to reinforce our sense of disenchantment. But as our living world increasingly rebels against the greed of humankind, and vigorously demonstrates both agency and power, we will increasingly find ourselves unable, and unwilling to remain in that debased state.

References

Descola, Philippe. 2013. Beyond Nature and Culture. Chicago: University of Chicago Press.

Douglas, Mary. 2002. Purity and Danger: An Analysis of Concepts of Pollution and Taboo. 1 edition. London ; New York: Routledge.

Lanier, Jaron. 2018. Ten Arguments For Deleting Your Social Media Accounts Right Now. 1st edition. London: Bodley Head.

Latour, Bruno. 2011. Waiting for Gaia. Composing the Common World through Arts and Politics. Lecture, French Institute.

Schneider, J. 1990. Spirits and the Spirit of Capitalism. *In* Religious Orthodoxy and Popular Faith in European Society. E. Badone, ed. Princeton: Princeton University Press.

Schrei, Joshua. 2023. Animism is Normative Consciousness - The Emerald Podcast. Accessed on Spotify on 08/11/2024.

Tocqueville, Alexis de. 2000. Democracy in America. HarperCollins.

Tylor, Edward. B. 1958. Religion in Primitive Culture. New York: Harper & Brothers Publishers.

Woolley, Jonathan. 2024. Orders of Magnitude: The Socio-Cultural Significance of Druidry for the English Landscape. *In* Modern Religious Druidry: Studies in Paganism, Celtic Identity, and Nature Spirituality. Ethan Doyle White and Jonathan Woolley, eds. Pp. 73–95.

MIRANDA L BARNES

The day the Moss first started to grow

Just a few tiny strands at first,
like billy goat hairs on a chin.
Hardly noticeable. But the patch
of ground at your feet grows warmer,
thicker, softer as you doze, sleep, bask,
and sleep again. You are still new
within your changed body. Rooted here
with arms outstretched, you are restful,
peaceful. The breeze just enough
to hold you there forever, growing
upwards between two balanced forces:
equal hungers for gravity and light.

The moss spreads, begins to tickle.
Deepens green from lemon-lime,
is the forest clock for time. It's touch
as delicate as a fawn's lips as she nibbles
one of your green buds. The moss
spreads over you like a blanket draped
lovingly upon a sleeping figure. Nothing
demanded, nothing possessed. You feed
from each other slowly, gently, always.
The forest clock is *always*, is ancient,
is without predilection. Is solace,
resurrection, unceasing benediction.

Homecoming

Auguries

You feed the birds each day
and have started taking your coffee at the table
looking out onto the back garden
every morning.

You have taken stock of which brood
has now grown to full flight,
give special attention to the sparrow
with the darker marking on his head

who is a little bigger, a little slower
than his siblings. You report on blackbirds,
their urgent, awkward running and strident
calls. When the robins were landing

on the empty birdhouse, we stood
at the glass, hoping they'd make their home
inside. Even pigeons and their scavenging
for seed are part of the choreography.

And you gently take away the pale
and featherless bodies of baby chicks
who have fallen from the nest
under the roof, near the garden gate.

You know the tenderness of loss.
Your father had an aviary,
and he taught you what you know of wings
before he found the sky.

RACHEL BENTHAM

Migrants

It was the sound of them that was so moving. Wisps of darkness gathered in the distant sky like smoke, then rushed towards me, blowing over fields and trees, then rising, turning suddenly upwards, all at once, in giant collective swoops. They flew in low, thousands of them, in fast-streaming clouds from all directions, undulating over the flatness of the Somerset levels. Murmuration – even the name focussed on the sound. It wasn't breath-taking, it was breath enhancing, creating a magical calm. As hundreds and thousands of delicate wings sliced gently through the air, they produced a sound like a long shivering sigh, as if the land itself exhaled with bliss. You had to be quiet to hear it; I was happy to be quiet. It had been raining all day, but now the sky had cleared and was washed with twilight pinks. A wide drainage channel below me glittered in the low evening light beside acres of tall reeds. The starlings moved as one, the way shoals of fish move in water, smoothly changing direction in great curving shapes above, bending to the invisible movements of air, billowing in grand, celebratory formations before dropping, as if suddenly exhausted, down into the reed beds. Apparently seven or eight million starlings altogether roosted there each night, six or more clinging to each reed in vertical dormitories. I wondered how and why they'd chosen reeds over trees, admiring their adaptability. As they disappeared into the reeds and settled, a low twittering buzz spread across the levels, somehow a comforting noise.

Small breakaway groups rose up out of the reeds, perhaps not happy with the most crowded areas, smoking upwards and resettling elsewhere. As the music of the settling starlings sifted through the cool evening air, more and more murmurations flew in from north and east and south, streaming overhead, then upsurging, twisting and bulging before dropping down to roost. The hugeness of the sky and the landscape stretched out all around. For these birds it had no borders; they could cross countries, seas, continents. How different their perspective on the landscape must be. Where did they come from tonight? Nearby towns and cities? How far did they fly each evening to reach this roost? Suddenly I remembered the starlings I'd raised as a child, forty years ago, when they were considered ugly, unwelcome immigrants, a threat to native ecologies, spreading across Europe in alarming, apparently threatening numbers.

That spring I'd broken my leg horse-riding, so it was encased in heavy plaster from toe to thigh. As the swelling and pain subsided, I began to stagger about. My father made me two small walking sticks, one a nice straight beech, and the other something twisty like hawthorn, a mini witch's stick. He got rubber bungs for the ends. It was easier to get about with these perfectly sized sticks rather than the unwieldy hospital crutches.

The broken leg meant I was housebound, unable to roam the woods, or climb trees, or call on my friends. Everyone else was at school, so my mother was not best pleased to have me at home. A while into my recovery, the woman next door had some work done in her loft, and as a result a nest of young starlings were evicted from the roof space. The parent birds were not in evidence. The four abandoned chicks were a sickly pink, with blue bulges for eyes and desperate gaping beaks. Scruffy tufts of feather sprouted through their transparent skin. The nest looked forlorn, marooned in the middle of an old wooden apple crate on the lawn next door. Our neighbour lamented as my mother and I leaned over the fence to look at them. 'I don't know what to do with them. Look at them; I can't bring myself to touch them. Horrible!'

Their heads wobbled as they craned blindly, perhaps waiting, hoping for their parents. They weren't pretty, fluffy chicks, but that wasn't the point. It seemed simple to me; they needed help.

'I'll look after them.'

The adults turned to me.

'Are you sure?' They seemed relieved.

'I'll find some worms or something to feed them.'

'They can't come in the house - they're probably full of fleas.' My mother nodded to the neighbour. 'It'll give her something to do, at least.'

No doubt everyone thought they would die. Given my existing menagerie of mice, a sink full of deformed tadpoles by the bins, plus our tortoise, two dogs and a cat, my parents may have considered death a favourable outcome. I was pragmatic rather than sentimental. As long as I could feed them often enough and keep the cat away from them more successfully than I kept him away from my cages of mice, they had a chance at least. The cat was canny; he'd worked out how to smash the glass lids of my mouse cages, pushing them off the shelves in the garage where they were housed, releasing the mice imprisoned within. Some had survived, some had not. I would have to be vigilant.

The baby starlings were handed over, still in the crate with the apple variety printed on the slats. They were duly named Cox, Orange, Pippin – and Teddybear. The miserable creature was nothing like a teddybear and there was no way I was inclined to cuddle it, but it was meant affectionately. I got some small pipettes, and attempted to feed the chicks every fifteen minutes with various mixtures of milk, bread, and mashed up worms. Small bald heads trembled on craning necks as they reached towards me, their open beaks forming four yellow diamonds of unending demand. Their eyes were closed, bluish lumps. They had no other options than my clumsy efforts.

It was kind of fun, squirting pipettes of mush into each beak again and again. I was determined to keep them alive. I searched the garden for worms and ruthlessly mashed them into a thick soup with milk until it was a squirtable consistency. The starlings were kept shut in the garage away from the cat and the dogs. I kept checking that the door was shut. Over and over, as the days progressed, I fed them. Who knows if I really managed to do it every fifteen minutes? Every half hour? I must have slept, as parent birds sleep. I took breaks to watch cheesy TV – the Wacky Races was a favourite, and The Golden Shot. When I returned to the nest in the garage, they began to open their eyes and look at me, their thoughts unfathomable. It wasn't long before their piping cries started up at my approach, as soon as I opened the garage door, as if I had become their giant mother starling. When I wasn't feeding them or looking for worms to mash, I learned to ride my bike with my plastered leg up on the handlebars, pedalling with my good foot, then freewheeling downhill at an exhilarating speed. I enjoyed this so much that a large hole was worn in the back of my plaster cast where it rubbed on the handlebars.

The days went by and the birds survived. They grew longer, smoother feathers. Their plumage improved their appearance, covering the vulnerability of their soft lumpy bodies and their thin, supplicatory necks, masking the contrast between their pink skin and bruise-coloured eye bulges. They got plumper, but they remained rather forlorn and tatty. They scrabbled with scratchy little claws to grip my finger. Their feathers were oddly hard to the touch, their bodies disturbingly light. Our long haired dachshunds were far more pleasant to touch. Unlike blue tits or owls or sparrows, even adult starlings weren't pretty to my eye, although their feathers were iridescent with subtle, changeable sheens of colour, like the rainbow shades that floated on the surface of petrol-greased puddles. Somehow neither starlings nor greasy puddles were allowed to be beautiful.

At some point during the baby birds' development, I watched a TV news item about the ongoing invasion of starlings. They'd spread across Europe from Russia and were not native to Britain. To demonstrate their numbers, a map of Europe was depicted, to which were added black dots, each representing a number of starlings – perhaps a thousand per dot. Anyway, the black dots were shown steadily obliterating each country as the sixties progressed and the starlings spread westwards, a dark cloud covering all visible land on the map, until they reached British shores, where they were threatening the habitats of native birds, making their noisy presence felt in town centres, defecating liberally wherever they gathered. My impression was that they definitely were not welcome. Migrants. It was the first time I'd heard the word. With their two clutches of eggs per year, both timed when insect populations were peaking, they were remarkably successful wherever they settled. Great clouds of them whirled up into the skies above city centres and countryside alike, performing their extraordinary murmurations, then roosting in chattering hordes in trees and tunnels and railway stations, strung out in ominous hundreds along telegraph wires. I also managed to watch Hitchcock's 'The Birds' around this time, which was terrifying.

I began to take the birds out into the garden to hop about on the grass. Eventually the cat got Cox, and possibly also Orange. It was hard to keep an eye on all four when they were outside. Pippin survived for a while then mysteriously died, collapsing beak first in a crumple of not quite fully grown feathers, hunched over like a very old man. Dead birds are stiff to touch. Birds do not wag tails with happiness to see you, or lick your hand as you bring worms and other unappetising treats. But they all got a decent funeral. There were no tears. Already I had been taught that emotion was something to be contained, if not successfully suppressed altogether.

Teddybear survived. Hobbling on my plaster cast, I taught him to fly by simply picking him up and launching him into the air. (I assumed he was a him without any evidence; back then animals were routinely referred to as male whatever their gender.) It might have looked as if I was throwing him, but there was affection in my attempts. Anyway, he managed to glide or flap to the ground, and later to perch on the garden fence. After a while he began to return and sit on my shoulder, ready for his next flight. He learned to fly well enough to keep out of range of the cat and the dogs, who watched his progress with hungry interest. The dogs consoled themselves by chewing the edges of the tortoise's shell as if it was a living bone. It was the seventies, tortoises were commonplace, and my parents didn't seem much concerned.

Teddybear sat on my shoulder as I excavated for worms. He also flew up into nearby trees, and then returned into my outstretched hands. After a while he stopped sleeping in his apple crate and roosted in trees near the house. Somehow he learned to find his own worms. Eventually, near the end of the summer, he disappeared. I didn't know if he'd died somewhere, or departed with the flocks migrating back to their winter quarters.

There was no discussion of this, my family being stoically pragmatic. I got on with reading Tolkien and starting secondary school, the former an escape from the miseries of the latter. I converted our old dolls house into luxurious new accommodation for my fast breeding mice. Once my cast was off, I had to strengthen my now withered leg with daily swimming, something I loathed. My grandmother offered me sixpence if I could swim a width without grimacing. I couldn't.

Homecoming

The following spring I was out in the garden burying one of my deceased mice. Possibly Reepicheep. I'd made him a golden casket out of the inside of an 'After-eights' chocolate box, which was laid in a shallow grave in my father's new rockery. I was instructed to bury dead mice underneath the large stones so that he wouldn't inadvertently dig them up again later. Anyway, after a dignified ceremony, I noticed a starling perching on the fence. One starling is very hard to distinguish from another, but starlings didn't usually land in that particular spot. It was too low, too dangerous. Only Teddybear had perched there when I was teaching him to fly. When I stood up and walked towards this bird, it didn't budge. Was it Teddybear?

As I approached, getting closer and closer, it just sat looking at me. Humbled, I thought about the huge distances each starling travelled. How could he possibly find the same area, the same street, the same garden, the same person? And how could he recognise me, despite my different clothes?

It was him. No other starling would let me come so close. He didn't fly to my shoulder, but we stood a long while looking at each other before he flew away. A yard apart. Where had he been – Russia, Africa? Far further than I had. He knew more of the world, and had incredible talents I would never have.

*

Forty years later, standing listening to the murmur of starlings roosting in the reed beds, I felt very small and ignorant in this giant landscape. The starlings knew it far better than I; they flew across miles of it every day, fed off it, inhabited its towns and cities, and found this rural roost each night. And they knew places in other countries too - their migrations took them to distant landscapes, other roosts. How did they decide where to go as they'd spread across Europe? I guessed that they chose the reed beds because they were safe. Suddenly I wondered if any of them fell off the reed to which they cling all night. Did any of them freeze and die? If so, no one would know. Would there be fish that ate them? I pictured small bodies, sodden in the water.

Now starling populations are decreasing, and any dismay at their initial arrival seems to be forgotten. They're regarded fondly as an asset rather than a threat. They're 'native' as well as migrant. We gather at dawn and dusk in fields and flatlands across Britain, oohing and aahhing as the shapes of whales, waves and teardrops gather and melt in the sky above us. The heart sighing sound of them is treasure.

NANCY M BELL

February's Breath

February's breath is caught
In the blue embrace of strengthening sky and sun
The fairy filigree of the tree's breath
Clings to their delicate fingers in frosty stillness

The exhalations of the earth and her children
Hang manifest in the blue silver air of early morning
Argent mist connecting field and sky
And binding all between them

The sky and wind reclaim the moisture
They lent to the earth in return
For the perfumes and bright colours
Of the prairie flowers and the dancing grain
Earth's children who partner the wind in summer's waltz

Here it begins in the chill breath of February
Bound beneath the iron frost and silent snow
The cold mist of earth reaches for the southern sun
Hanging in pearlescent drifts over the crystal snow

Voices whispering among the dry grasses
Soft sigh of the drifting snow
where the wind sifts it like sugar
sacred geometry figures fleeting over snowy crust

February's breath pregnant with the promise of spring

November Ice

Tiny crystals spin and weave
As the temperature dips and freezes
Icy webs that catch the light
Of the baby moon climbs the heights
Lace that spreads as a lady's skirts
Builds a skim of silver that flirts
Along the edges of the still water
Spins and weaves until later
The icy silver weaving holds the snow
Above the living water below

HELEN SMITH

reincarnation

I have been here before, on these flagstones
beside the fireplace now charcoal and woodlouse nest

I have been here on two legs
when I hung my coat on the peg, and sank deep
into the armchair now green with moss
and soft with decay

I inch towards it, one leg after the other
after the other
it feels further now
and the wind is a cold river from the door

last time I was here, I had to stoop to enter
now my feet find the silence between dust and stone
and the ivy that has crept from the forest

before, when summer was promised
on the morning breeze
I swept cobwebs from the mantle
laughing, at something someone had said

Homecoming

I didn’t pause to feel the spider’s body crush
under my heel, the cricket’s leg snap
as I swept it over the doorstep

I tuned out the moth’s wing
beating against the trap
as darkness swallowed day
and the fire drew me to its warmth

I smiled a lot, then

and now, sometimes, I can still smell
the place where my body lay
crooked for three days before it was found

I thought I was not part of the forest
I thought I could not inhabit xylem and haemolymph
articulated bodies, funnel webs
and soil-blind fungal unbecoming

I did not know the wild in the shedding cells
of my skin, and the thin paper
of the wasps nest I shook from the rafters
shivered to the same wind’s tune

I reach the chair, smell fox on the upholstery
blink six of my eight eyes
and I start to spin

naked, animal

I want to roll naked in the soil
let the skin of my body meet
the skin of the earth
become the animal that I am
I want to move like a wild thing, soft
undulations, feeling, sensing, exploring
I want my body to be a portal to pleasure
connection
sensation through every pore
animal, loving the earth with the pads of my feet
with every step
with every fluid motion let my spine find its rhythm
along the backbone of the earth
I want to breathe the sky
and let my breath co-mingle with the breath
of all beings
in this more-than-human world
I may be naked and domesticated
but my soul is a woodland creature
unfurling at the caress of the sun
nerve fibres sparkling, a dance of aliveness
belonging to the scent of damp earth
I want to be awake to it all
awake
to the pulse of life
human, animal
let the separation melt and let me flow like

Homecoming

rivers
to the core of what it means to be alive
to the cosmic beating, moving, breathing
energy
ecology
let me roll naked in the soil
and let the landscape of my body know
that it belongs

KATE HAWKEY

The Indian Bean Tree

We walk

Looking for shade

Between busy by-pass and the road which takes the football traffic

Looking to screen out the noise

Of people in a hurry, the world in chase

We find a connection of trees. Inside, the grass is still cool green despite the heat and lack of rain

On one side is an upturned bike and a woman doing repairs

On the other is Jade's Garden, a memorial to an ecologist who died too young

A mum arrives with baby and dog
H smiles at the baby busy eating daisies
They catch each other's eye and play a waving game

The dog responds and brings a slobbered stick in anticipation

Homecoming

We talk about what makes us feel
safe, daily rituals to steady the anxiety
of a future arriving too soon

We lie on the grass, follow the arc of
the slow blue sky, still tethered

As we step back out into the sun

The Indian bean tree announces itself
with heady scent

And floral stage of dancers doing the
can-can

How to draw a crowd

When time allows

Its twisting trunk looks back towards
the trees in the estate parkland

To a time before the by-pass

Its helical spin reaches further across
the ocean

To a land before dislocation

A past embedded into the ground

Still held, secure

GORDON MACLELLAN

Holding Treasure

I am a storyteller: I work with words all the time and try to use them carefully, so when a word like “nature” comes along, a word with so many possible meanings and interpretations, I find myself intrigued, trying to untangle possibilities, and gently weaving threads of meanings into a new braid.

The poet, magician, wordsmith in me holds “nature” like a fragment of treasure, turns it over, weighs it, measures it, considers how it fits *here*, how its meaning changes, *there*, wonders if anyone will notice. In poems, spells, invocations, words are chosen carefully, used precisely like fine-honed blades. But “nature” confuses. It holds so many facets, an insect’s compound eye, offering many slightly different images of the same thing. Spoken, written, recited, chanted or sung, what does “nature” bring, who does it invoke, what does it bind, who does it hold, what does it separate?

Because for some people that thought of “nature” implies separation, implies an “us” and “everyone else” situation. This then informs a whole “nature connection” industry (that some of us have spent years exploring as environmental education). Surely “connection” is a constant? There is no escape, no separation. But if by “connection” we mean understanding, empathy, appreciation, then there is a distance to respond to.

My neat braid is starting to fray.

And then for still other people “nature” implies something precious, a wonder, a richness that we may or may not have access to but that calls for protection and celebration. Or then again "nature" may simply be a resource to exploit, a set of "ecosystem services" to quantify and use as we see fit.

My braid coils, becomes a knot, grows tighter.

Most of my everyday work is about encouraging people to explore creatively their relationship with the world around them and to reflect on their place within it. For that process, "nature" with all its mixed meanings is useful. It is a starting point that most people recognise: sometimes as something good, sometimes as something they don't like, sometimes as a distance. The valuable element is that it can help start the discussion. As a word, it encourages exploration of an idea.

I think for most people, "nature" is more straightforward. It is the only word people have to embrace the richness around them. "Nature" encompasses the world we live in. It includes concepts like biodiversity, and ecosystems and ecological processes. There may be discussion around the recognition of the "man-made world" as part of "nature". There may be debate about our relationship with "nature" but usually "we're part of it"is the understanding. We may be a bit wayward, misbehaving, but we are still part of it all and other words or scientific or jargon terms are not really helpful.

The animist in me doesn't really mind what we think "nature" means. For that animist self, it is the feeling that matters, the experience that runs through "*natura*", the essence – the nature - of a thing: an individual, an idea, a whole ecosystem. Here, our use and concern over words is in danger of missing the experience. Whatever words we use, or disapprove of: nature, environment, biodiversity, wildlife, we need to remind ourselves that these are words and while they describe, they do not contain the experience of the world we live in. We should not let the words get in the way of being part of it.

Homecoming

In the end, like most language discussions, I don't think there is a definitive stance to take on "nature" but what does matter for me in my strongest self is "respect". However we describe the world we are part of (recognising richness, treasures, connection and all) the most important quality is respect. Living with respect for the other beings we share this world with, respect for the dynamic processes that this world vibrant, beautiful and alive, and a simple respect for the world as it holds us….

And now, I'll pick up this tangled ball, that knotted hedgerow of words, carry it out, set it down and let the world do what it will with it.

London Square

A plane tree,
As tall as the church tower,
Tucks neatly in
Between the spire and the office block ,
And the traffic,
And the shops,
And the buses,
And the people,
And the noise.
Grass grows quietly,
Flowers invite a bumblebee feast,
Trees spread shade,
Offer welcome.
Wrestling, children kill each other on the lawn
While oblivious pigeons strut past, courting.

Homecoming

There are always corners,
Wild corners where the foxes play,
Where the rats dance,
Where urban butterflies thrive
And gossiping sparrows gather.
These are wild places.
No-one has ever convinced the trees they are not free.
Here, I am uplifted.
And the pigeons remain oblivious.

GRAHAM HARVEY

Why its Ok for Vegan Animists to Kill Slugs

2024 has been a good year for slugs in the UK. But not such a good year for gardeners. A mild wet spring was a delight to slugs who proceeded to chomp their way through whatever vegetation they fancied. This is, of course what they've been doing for millennia. But in the previous year there hadn't been so many slugs.

There's a strawberry patch in a small bit of the planet that I call "my allotment". I doubt slugs see it that way even though they've co-evolved their lifestyles alongside our (human) evolution of "gardens". Anyway, 2023 was a great year for strawberries. There were plenty for us to eat fresh and in crumbles (usually with allotment-grown rhubarb). We gave lots to neighbours, and froze to eat through the winter. The slugs ate quite a few – and that was fine. Indeed, towards the end of summer I stopped harvesting strawberries and let our other-than-human kin enjoy their feasts.

This year was different. Not just in the strawberry patch. Slugs ate all the emerging courgette plants. They went for young dahlias and delphiniums. OK, to the point. I've been vegan since the mid-1980s, and I probably first called myself an animist in the 1990s. When I'm asked how I deal with slugs, the question seems loaded. I'm clearly supposed to have found a way to coexist harmoniously with the slimy voracious critters. I have tried. When I say that I evict some from the garden, that seems ok. But when I say that I have also resorted to beer traps (slugs love cheap lager, but it kills them) and now use the "slug killer pellets" labelled ok for organic gardening, I seem to surprise, shock or upset my interrogators. It seems that killing slugs is either "not vegan" or "not animist" or both.

I think what's going on is that people really do not think that I – or any other human – is part of "nature". They say we are, but I don't think they mean it. I think they are still trapped in the culture/ nature, human / environment dualism. People have told me that its ok for hedgehogs and thrushes to kill slugs because that's "natural". To be clear, these conversations are always about killing, never about eating. No-one says "it'd be ok if you ate them".

I chose to eat strawberries, courgettes, carrots and cauliflowers (I could go on) and that seems ok. Well, yes, there are people who think that not eating cows isn't natural, but I'm not in the least interested in hearing that rant again, thanks. However, in order to eat what I chose to eat I must compete with slugs. I have tried to ask them to share. I've tried to ask caterpillars not to eat all the cabbages. I plant extra so that sharing is possible. But that only works if there's restraint on both sides.

So sometimes I resort to violence against my competitors. This, it seems, isn't ok. I'm not supposed to do what is ok in the "nature" that is hedgehogs, thrushes and nematodes. I'm supposed to leave some kinds of killing to them. Maybe it doesn't matter that I'm vegan – I don't know any carnivores or omnivores who eat slugs. And even if I ate cows as well as carrots I'd still be struggling with the voracity of slugs and other pesky creatures. Not many other people (vegans included) think that carrots might be sentient enough not to want to be eaten. The desires and ambitions of vegetables are rarely taken into consideration. So perhaps it only matters that I'm an animist. Perhaps people think animism is about living nicely alongside all other lives. But that's romanticism not animism. In the real world, animism involves acts of violence.

Does it help if I quote my favourite definition of a religion? The late Māori scholar, Te Pakaka Tawhai, said "the purpose of religious activity is doing violence with impunity". He illustrates this with kumara, sweet potatoes. Because kumara migrated to Aotearoa alongside Māori, and because they are grown with effort, care and respect, harvesting and eating kumara is an act of intimate but necessary violence. It involves taking the lives of other-than-human kin. Just as I take the lives of carrots and other veg. Let's be clear: "doing violence with impunity" does not mean "do a quick ritual and everything is permitted". Tawhai wrote about religion or ceremony as purposeful activity, as work, and places it at the heart of negotiating complex relationships.

So, a bit like traditional Māori growers of kumara, my allotment work includes the purposeful activity of seeking permission and offering placation, saying please, sorry and thanks. If anything is "natural", it doesn't matter whether slugs are killed by hedgehogs and thrushes or by me. But the varied interactions between me, slugs, strawberries and hedgehogs are all cultural relationships. The allotment is an animistic community, enlivened by the purposeful pursuit of good living, replete with etiquettes of respect, and shaped by some limitations on what one or another being is free to do. Being kin cannot mean that I have to welcome everyone to do as they will. *Sometimes* it is ok to kill slugs.

THERESA KELLEHER

Still Intact

Out of nowhere
the large
white feather
appeared.
Two hands long,
scars across and down,
one section shorn,
yet still intact.
Downy fondrills
splay from the
once was quill.
Curved from the hip
touch as light as the
morning breeze,
shimmering silver.
I'm swept off my feet
into a swelling of
heartfelt, delicate beauty.
Sensing the
flow and the
rhythm of change,
I look within and
explore the stars.
I listen to the voice that is
soundless.
'With every ending
there is a beginning'.

FRANK OLDING

Cadno

Creulonach ddiwedd Tachwedd
y gwynt sy’n fflangellu’n gwedd.
Eisoes addewir cesair;
ar gerddinen medd hen air
aeron sy’n ernes eira
a rhaid ar ddefaid, ar dda.

Gan olrhain er dwyreinwynt
yn ddi-raen ar glawdd ryw hynt,
tuthia draw heb fraw, heb frys,
yn wystl rhy fain ei ystlys
i eira, rhew a newyn
yn heth y gweundiroedd hyn.

Dwyglust anniben cenau
yn fawr o hyd a rhy frau;
a’i lond o lefrith dan lwyn
yn genau yn y gwanwyn,
dôi’r gadnöes, ffres ei phrae,
i herio’i chnud i chwarae.
Ond chwelir rhith ei frith fro
ar esgyll gwynt afrosgo
a’r ddrycin a’i gerwinder
a fling ei gynffon yn flêr.

Yn ei angen, ni’m cenfydd;
yn ei raid, sylw ni rydd
i’r un a ddaw ar ei ôl,
ysir ei reddf gynoesol
gan ing ei gythlwng a’i gno

a'i gyni nad yw'n gwanio.
Ni ŵyr, a'i holl synhwyrau
yn swrth, fy mod yn nesáu.

Rhagom, er cryfed ffromwynt,
yn awr yma gwyra'r gwynt.
O glywed ôl arogl dyn,
sadia, try'i ben yn sydyn –
marciau'i safn fel dagrau du
a'i lygaid o'i hir lwgu
yn fawr oll, yn grwn gan fraw;
yn ei hast, ond yn ddistaw,
o'i glawdd hed fel llucheden,
ar ei ôl yr heliwr hen.

Fox

Crueller at November's end
in our faces scourging wind.
Promise already of hail;
on rowan, says old lore,
berries are sure sign of snow,
of dire need on flock, on herd.

Despite east wind, he tracks
some scent along a wall
and trots unhurried, unafraid,
a hostage all too gaunt his flank
to snow and ice and famine
in this bitter upland.

He still has scruffy cub's ears,
too big, too frail;
safe in brake and full of milk,

a cub in spring,
the vixen brought fresh prey
to dare her young to play.
Illusions of a dappled hollow
scatter on the clumsy wind,
rough weather, storming,
flays his ruffled tail.

In his need, I go unseen,
in his want, he pays no heed
to one behind him,
primeval instinct blunt
with hunger, the gnaw
of long, unfailing hardship.
All his senses sluggish,
I close in unsensed.

In our faces, for all its fury,
here, now, wind shifts.
Scenting man,
he stands, he turns his head –
his snout-marks like black tears,
his eyes from long starvation
big, round with terror;
in his haste, but silent,
he bolts like lightning off his wall,
the ancient hunter at his heels.

JON NASH

Back to Nature

I don't want to get back to nature.
Or hug a tree.
I want to slip wordlessly
Between the folds of
Its rough bark
And circle the rings around
Its heartwood.
I want to grow
Lightning bolt branches
And feel the sun on my crown.
Stretch my fingers
Into its leaves
And breathe from them.
Plunge my feet between its
Roots and drink
From ancient aquifers.
Let my nervous system
Turn mycelian
And spread out in
The underworld of soil and silence.
I want to lose myself
In its slow time and
Sun blessed stretching.
Count time in temperature
And light.

Homecoming

Feel my thoughts turn to chlorophyll
And my blood to thick sap
And feel my own skin
Twist and harden
As I sense the gentle drop
Of a robin on my arm.

CERRI LEE

Autumn Equinox: a Ritual Memory

The heavy grey clouds drift slowly seaward across the South Downs having had their say in the sharp language of thundery showers, their grim countenance now broken in places allowing pale blue sky to peer through and offer vague promises of sunshine. Far below, gathering under the rain soaked ponderous trees, the community watches the glowering skies with cautious optimism. Perhaps the weather gods will be kind. There is a growing sense of anticipation with each new arrival. There are cheerful greetings for familiar faces, laughter, barking dogs and children's eager voices ringing around the picnic area as the space is readied for the festivities.

At some point before the ritual almost everyone steals a moment to lean on the wooden rail and quietly commune with the figure of the Long Man. His featureless face seems to gaze benevolently over the fields beneath his feet and this assembly of likeminded souls. No-one knows how long he has watched over this land. How many harvests must he have presided over whilst stood as sentinel to the ancestors residing in the barrows above his head?

All are drawn back to the company when the call for volunteers to take speaking parts goes up. By 2pm the various roles have been assigned and each participant studies their part. At the centre of the circle the Harvest Basket sits full with ripe offerings brought from our gardens, allotments. A symbol of the harvest season, a cornucopia of vegetables, fruits and flowers. The Rooks above seem to notice and in a flurry of wings send up a chorus of rasping calls. The Rooks will take turns with other birds to bring a continuous accompaniment of birdsong throughout the ritual. From the start this ritual feels deeper, more intense than usual. We are here right on the time of Equinox and the thrumming energy of transition is palpable.

The incense is lit as a few late comers trot breathlessly across the grass to join hands with the circle.

It is time.

A reverential hush falls across the space as the circle forms. Hand in hand around the harvest altar, we take a long slow breath together, drawing into ourselves the energy of the earth beneath our feet. With another long slow breath we open to the infinite sky, acknowledging the vital breath within. A third deep breath aligns our heartbeat to the rivers, streams and seas, the life blood pulsing through our sacred island. All thoughts of our fractious journeys and everyday cares fall away in these conscious breaths. We stand fully present in the moment, harmony radiating through the company and filling this precious place.

We call for there to be peace throughout the world, for without peace no work can be. The circle is cast and blessed. The Druid's prayer is spoken. The Awen is sung. And so we are cocooned in a world of enchantment, myth and memory. The elemental energies and spirits of place are invited to join us and witness our rite, as we offer gratitude for this year's harvest of earthy delights. We are open to the elements, to the spirits of place and to each other. We are ready to celebrate this turn on the Wheel of Life.

The Herald strides forward to the centre of the circle and plants his staff and issues forth with full voice. "As Orion crests the horizon and strides into the night sky the deer begin to rut in fields and woodland. The land responds to lengthening shadows with the crisp earthy smells of early autumn, we see the slow drift toward a much needed rest begin. The sunlight spills as liquid gold across the earth. The harsh summer sun now passed, its glory diminished. We remember how in Spring we were breathless for every new height achieved. We waited with bated breath as new flowers and crops were coaxed into life. The joy of life reborn ran through the birdsong and into the hearts of all. With our memories of growth and light we now stand at the Autumn Equinox and the energy of this celestial tipping point is palpable. Amid these trees we look up and see their countenance shifting from the deep green of high summer to the sultry beauty of autumn's glory. All life is preparing for the long sleep to come. The anticipated harvest has been gathered and stored to see us through the dark nights to come.

Today we take our time to give thanks and celebrate the hard-won gifts of the land, but also those harvests of mind, body and spirit. It is time to show our gratitude for the bounty of the waxing times, to remember the traditions of the past with an eye to the future, just as our ancestors have done since we made a sacrificial God of the wheat and the corn. The cry has gone up, the race is run, the last cut has been made in fields of wheat and barley. There is a call that still echoes in the memories of many, 'I have the neck and we shall have our bread, for John Barleycorn is dead.' So, now the corn dollies will be woven from his bones and be welcomed to sit beside our hearths. As we look at them we will remember the nature of all the sacrifices made to bring us through the ravening dark of winter." The Herald melts back into the circle leaving his potent words to ring in our hearts.

A storyteller's voice rises as she sweeps into view, radiant in her countenance with corn gold hair.

"I speak for the Corn Dolly, a spirit of the Harvest. I am a child of memory formed from the stalks and seed heads of John Barleycorn. Weave me into life from his sacrificial bones. My true spirit lies within the seeds you keep, those that will be sown when the seasons and the tides turn once more. As you twist and knot brittle stalks to give me shape and form I will sing of arcane knowledge gleaned from every season. I will offer insights occult and ancient allowing you to glimpse the secret held in the heart of every seed. If my knowledge is what you seek then give me a place of honour at your hearth, keep me safe all through the autumn and the winter hours.

Winter will come in the guise of the Raven Queen to rattle the roof tiles and shake the trees. Pull close your blanket and hide as it stalks the land and I will sing to you the soul-song of Old John Barleycorn. Each new Corn Dolly is tasked to weave new threads onto the tapestry of life. Contained within our song is the story of the land. Each new memory becomes a harmony, each harmony conjures an image to be woven into the fabric of time and space. Our song is endless, it ensures nothing is lost but is carried seamlessly into the future, as it rides on echoes of the past. We sing a tale as old as the hills, yet it is always vital and sweet as a child's first breath.

And so, we slide gracefully, even gratefully, into Autumn's mists and mellow fruitfulness. We move with joyful voices full of appreciation for the gift of life and the grace it leaves as it passes. Take a moment now to review the fruits of your harvest. What gifts are concealed at its heart, be that a harvest of earthly delights or of harvests of the heart, mind or spirit? Find the seeds held deep within each fruitful moment of this waxing year." She invites the company to close our eyes and gives us a few moments to reflect on our waxing year's journey. We turn inward to feel the journey and search for our own personal harvest. Softly she calls us from memory and says, "I invite you to join me in honouring those fresh new seeds. Repeat after me, if you are willing."

We follow her lead in call and response as we chant:

With the blessing of Water, Air and Earth,
Each harvest brings a bounty,
With joyous heart and grateful grace,
We dance toward the darkness.

Gracefully, the spirit of the Corn Dolly withdraws, making way for the whispering Spirit of Autumn to come forward.

Homecoming

She embodies our sense of Autumn - a kaleidoscope of colours reflecting the ever-changing canopy of leaves above. With sultry voice she conjures images of carefree children who chase the spiralling leaves as they drift into golden drifts: "I speak for the spirit of Autumn. The land turns its face from the sun and drifts slowly toward the dreaming. But, there is still time for you to take in the aromas of the earth's richness and be awed by the beauty of its transformation. It has been said that the trees have a unique art and poetry in their language of transition. They gracefully catch every nuance in the dying of the light as their green leaves shift through hues of red, yellow, russet and gold. For that dazzling gift every year we all might stand in gratitude and in profound awe. Soon those leaves will fall, chased into piles and drifts by chill breezes. Those whistling winds sweep away the outworn without malice nor any ill-will.

They carry out this task with a surety of purpose and great panache in a swirling shower of colours. Observing this festival we sense the ebbing energy of one journey and the beginning of another.

But this is no time for melancholy. Rather it is time to run like children and chase the dancing leaves as they fall into deepening shadows. This is an opportunity to gather in, count up and cherish all the joys and the sorrows of another fruitful season. Allow yourself to revel in the adventure so far and busy yourself by laying down stores for the dark times ahead.

Autumn's magic is held in the honeyed light falling across the hills. As those shadows deepen the world seems more vibrant, even more defined against the green gold of the landscape. Trees in their mantle of rustling leaves are bejewelled with ripening fruit, they strike a last dramatic pose before that sweet moment of release, as the last fruits fall, their task will be complete.

Life is an infinitely complex notion, an eternal mystery which we can never fully understand until the journey's end. But, the wise know that nothing ever truly ends. When the seasons have turned new seeds will find their feet in fresh new soil, soil fed by all that has gone before. When we appreciate and honour these cycles of life and death we pave the way for rebirth. Every bite of this harvests holds a sweet memory to savour. Take a moment now to feel the seeds of this harvest, both of the earth and of the mind." She gives us time to feel the new seeds we harbour in our hearts and minds.

Then she says: "Repeat after me, if you are willing."

We are willing, and chorus we do:

I am the ripening fruit,
In my heart a seed has formed.
I embrace the season's ebb and flow,
And from the darkness will be reborn.

A spiralling leaf, she dances back into the circle as we contemplate the magic we are weaving. These are affirmations, spells to bind and hold us to our own account. These are not idle expressions in a whimsical moment, these are promises made to honour the hard-won gifts of this growing season and the land, the trees, and the birds calling above us stand as witnesses. If we feel any pressure or doubt in making these commitments, those worries ease as the gentle voice of the World Tree issues forth, casting yet another softly woven spell over the circle. The lilting voice crafts images of deep roots and wide open branches and the notion of worlds within worlds filling our mind's eye as she speaks.

"I speak for the World Tree. Oh, how I feel you, those brash winds of change! You come whistling through my boughs, and welcome! Though you whip and tear away each leaf or fruit sending them tumbling, I bear you no malice. Strip me bare for all I care! When you roar I will dance, when you are gentle I shall sway. You can never hold me back from my stout purpose, neither do you hamper the progress of the things I hold sacred. I am grateful for you, you rejuvenate, revitalise and reinvigorate.

Homecoming

To those with little understanding I stand alone, a sad solitary tree in a bare field, yet for those who look deeper, they will see I harbour worlds within worlds. I am a nurturer of generations! A myriad generations of birds and beasts have called me their home, they all keep me company. All manner of fleeting existence has lived, loved, nurtured their young, and passed on, trusting the next generation to continue their song. Stories and memories echo within these branches.

I am a whole universe unto myself. I am a city, a deep rooted oasis offering sanctuary to the multitudes as the desert encroaches. Through the descending dark and the rising light, throughout the heat of summer and the rattling rains I hold them safe, just as the earth holds me. I once touched branch to branch and root to root with many who have long since tumbled and faded, yet I am never alone for their memories are in my heartwood. This landscape is constantly changing, but I hold its story safe in my roots.

So blow you winds of change, bring on the darker days, the frosts, the rain, and through it all I will stand naked and silent, for I am a World Tree. My roots are deep. They reach into the realm of dreams where might I fly on Raven wings or scuttle across the earth on dainty beetle pins. Rooted I may be, unable to stride over the horizon, yet always I am as free as the throng of life sleeping in my crooks and nooks, together in slumber our dreams entwine. Tell me, how are your roots and branches, are they strong yet flexible enough to move with the winds of change?"

"Yay!" We chorus, riding on the power of her enchantment.

"Then," she says, "repeat after me, if you are willing:"

My roots reach deep,
As my branches open wide,
My body holds true as I embrace these shifting skies.

Homecoming

As the chant subsides around the circle the World Tree withdraws leaving us fully committed to our vows and affirmations.

Time now for our Bards to take the stage and offer their creative gifts to the spirits of time, place and community. As each one comes forward to share a seasonal tale we are enthralled. There is laughter the occasional gasp as stories twist and turn. As the tales are spun we enjoy a feast, honey biscuits and fruit drinks. When the last Bard's tale is done and the feast all consumed, we feel the weather gods impatience, a damp tip-tapping as the grey clouds loom once more.

The Herald strides back into the circle to firmly plant his dragon-topped staff. His clear voice calling us to order. Gazing around the circle he asks us to consider these questions.

"Are we grateful for our earthly harvests?"

"We are," comes the response.

"Are we ready to weave deep magic from the bones of this year's harvest?"

"Oh yes!" the circle replies.

The Herald is not convinced of our commitment, claiming in pantomime style that he cannot hear us. With gales of laughter we gave him our best, "Oh yes!"

With this effort he seems satisfied, and with a last sweep of his eye about the circle he calls: "Do we feel the strength of the World Tree within us, those deep roots and wide branches? And are we willing to nurture those seeds of inspiration, of magic, and new life that now lie within us?"

With full enthusiastic voices, we confirm that this is so.

"Then, my most marvellous Anderida Druids, we are ready to journey into the dark nights and embrace the seasons of rest and recuperation. So we call to the power of the Stag in the heat of the chase and the magical White Hind. May they be our guides through the Autumn mists as we walk into the dreaming. May this harvest sustain our bodies. May the Corn Dollies inspire our minds with their magical memory, and the World Tree hold our spirits with its strength of purpose on our continuing journey."

The Herald raises his staff and sweeps back into the circle.

The ritual is almost complete. We thank the spirits of place and unwind the circle dissolving the cocoon of enchantment about us. Before we leave this sacred place, we have one last conscious task. We stand in our communal circle hand in hand to acknowledged and give thanks once more to the waxing half of the year. Then, as one, we turn to face outwards to imagine the enfolding dark before us. Here on this Equinox, at the tipping point, we feel the energy of the waxing year behind us and the waning year waiting open armed. With hearts and minds full of treasures, we consciously step forward into the enfolding dark. The Rooks rise up and caw their approval, a silent Barn Owl sweeps across the field before us as a drizzle of rain begins to fall. We pack everything away leaving only echoes. As we leave, a flock of Geese fly over, no doubt heading for warmer climes. Autumn has arrived, the energy has shifted, all the worlds seem to have heard our words, and we feel truly blessed.

HANNAH WILLOW

Home

The stars shimmer behind my eyes
And the bright moon curves into my
heart.

My bones are the dust of my
ancestors
And grass grows under my skin.

Green leaves flutter in my ears,
And mountain streams flow in my
veins.

My feet track the land and
remember, remember.

The song of the night birds rings in
my voice
And I feel the footsteps of bears and
badgers in my soul

As the night sky slowly turns
I feel them all
And know that I am home.
I am home.

ANDREW ANDERSON

Nature and the Terror of Connection

I have been spending quite a lot of time recently reflecting on the fact that there is something about Nature which I find instinctively and yet gratifyingly terrifying.

For such a simple sentence, that introductory line needs a lot of unpacking. Firstly, let us start with the concept of Nature. As an animist, defining nature is quite a hard thing to do. Potentially, everything is Nature because everything is produced by Nature. Even things like sky-scrapers, motorways and credit cards could be considered as Nature because they are produced by humans, which are part of Nature. However, for the sake of this article, let us define Nature as anything that is part of the non-human world. Even that definition is somewhat ambiguous. While it clearly delineates tigers, basking sharks and oak trees as Nature, what about those beings involved in human-based activities such as farming? Are the wheat and sheep in the fields Nature? Well, for the sake of this article, yes, although it is important to note that they are Nature which, these days, are caught in an un-natural and industrialised process.

The way in which that world is "instinctively and yet gratifyingly terrifying" is going to take a lot longer to unpack.

To begin, I think it is worth considering that there is a tradition of thinkers and philosophers who have found something innately terrifying in Nature. People have been finding Nature a bit scary for years.

Perhaps the most obvious instance of this way of thinking is in the concept of the Sublime as seen in philosophical and literary works from the seventeenth to nineteenth-centuries. The Sublime shows Nature to be beautiful and horrifying in equal measure. In fact, it is the beauty of Nature which is so overwhelming, so beyond the comprehension of the human mind, that it instinctively fills us with a sense of horror. However, there is a problem relating how I feel with the concept of the Sublime. The Sublime is and was generally triggered by the human mind experiencing something incomprehensible, such as a range of mountains or a sweeping vista. It is generally connected to scale, showing the mightiness of the hand of God. A sense of unease caused by engagement with Nature on our doorstep does not fit with this experience.

While considering that sense of unease, it is also worth briefly acknowledging the sense of the Uncanny. While this term addresses a sense of being ill at ease, it does not quite fit the idea I am exploring here. With the Uncanny, there is a sense of something being oddly familiar, with the fright coming from a sense of recognition. I do not think I am terrified by something I recognise but rather something that I cannot quite grasp, something other. And do not forget that I described this emotion as a “gratifying” terror. In other words, it is an emotion which ultimately, I like. It is a feeling which has drawn me closer to Nature, not scared me away.

Like many animists (and, you could argue, most people in general) many of my strongest childhood memories revolve around my connection to Nature. If you believe Rousseau, that is because children are inherently closer to Nature, uncorrupted by the sin of human society. There might be something in that. I remember crawling around on the floor as a child with the family cats and dogs just as fondly that I do engaging with the human members of my family or neighbours. As far as I was concerned, people could have four legs as well as two – until I was taught that was not the case. Family members only have two legs, apparently.

I was lucky enough to be raised on an estate which had good access to natural spaces. At the bottom of our road were extensive Celtic earthworks over which trees had grown. Groups of us would often descend upon the woodland to play there, so I grew up being in natural and wild spaces. But there was something in those woods that I was always a little bit afraid of, which I could never put my finger on. All I knew is that it was something not human. The fear I felt was not enough to drive me out of the woods but it was something which kept me on my toes. It was something that, somehow, made me feel more alive.

I knew that the fear was not connected to the animal life in the woods because I had been in there often enough to know that there was nothing of any size which lived there permanently. In fact, the scariest animal I ever saw in there was a mole, and that was only scary because I was not expecting to see one and was unsure what I should do to help it (in the end I did nothing and left mole to his own doings). Neither was the fear connected to the smaller creepy crawlies of the space. Ok, so my definition of family at that stage did not extend as far as those with eight legs but I considered those with six legs to be friendly neighbours. No, what I was afraid of was something much bigger and more nebulous.

I remember feeling the same sense of unease in a classroom one day. Again, I was lucky to go to a school which was surrounded by open, natural spaces and with plenty of wildlife, but I distinctly remember my teacher putting a display of teasels, honesty and other dried hedgerow plants on the windowsill and something deep inside me was a bit uneasy about them. I could not explain why, I just knew what I felt.

It is probably important to acknowledge at this stage that I was born in the early 1970s, so the period I am describing here would probably cover the late 1970s and early 1980s. Although I remember this as a golden period where I was deeply connected to Nature, it is probably just as true to say that, objectively, children of this period were not as connected to Nature as the generation before. It is probably a form of Shifting Baseline Syndrome where gradual changes are accepted as normal because human experience is subjectively limited to our own lifespan. While I remember playing in the woods a lot, I also remember playing with *Star Wars* toys and watching a lot of TV, so my childhood probably did not include as much Nature as, say, that of my parents.

It is also important to consider how Nature was presented in culture at that time. As a child interested in the natural world, I used to seek out TV shows and pictures of animals in books and on walls. One of the strongest visual memories I have is of a set of steak plates from the 1970s which were decorated with pictures of different bulls. Each plate showed a creature that was abstracted and angular, painted with greens, pinks and blues. There was nothing natural about them and yet I loved them. Were these images simply part of 1970s consumer culture or was there something deeper and more primal going on there? Abstracting creatures for art is nothing new. While the images on those steak plates look very much of their time, there is something about them which reverberates with the cave paintings of the aurochs in Lascaux.

One of the definitive presentations of Nature for my generation was the 1978 film *Watership Down*. The film opens with animation as abstracted as that on those steak plates. The story of Frith and El-arairah, the deity and ancestor of all rabbits, is told before the main action of the film begins. And while the animation of the main film is stunningly beautiful and incredibly realistic, it is shot through with a sense of darkness and menace. Yes, there are plenty of scenes set in the daytime but there are also darkened corners, landscapes obscured by fog and fields running red with blood. It is a film about threat, dislocation and loss. *Watership Down* is more like a folk horror than a Disney movie which my poor sister, who had to carry me from the cinema, traumatised and screaming, did not understand when she took me see it.

So, do I find Nature terrifying because I grew up in the 1970s, was more dislocated from the natural world than I realise and was taken to see a scary film about rabbits? Well, it is possible, I suppose, but I think it all goes a bit deeper than that. What I would like to suggest is that 1970s steak plates and the film *Watership Down* did not simply make Nature frightening for an impressionable child but were part of a longer tradition which 'othered' the natural world and those humans who lived close to it.

This othering of Nature was driven by several factors: religion, industrialisation and consumerism. For example, with the rise of Protestantism in the 1600s, people who lived closer to Nature and were skilled in natural crafts found themselves labelled as witches and were punished as such. A population fearful of such accusations were driven into the arms of the church and told that God, rather than the natural world, would provide for them. Creatures such as toads, rats, cats and ravens were seen as being in league with the devil or being the devil incarnate. Following the acts of enclosure, generations were driven off the land and into towns where the wages from work in the factories provided for one's family, not the land. And why rely on natural herbal remedies to cure your ills when someone in a shop or on the internet could sell you a solution instead? Ultimately, all of this is driven by the need for power and control over others, replacing the support they receive from Nature with the products provided by the people in power.

A look at art during this period sees a shift in the way Nature is presented. Looking at woodcuts from the medieval period, we see the Devil not in human form but as a beast, black and shaggy with horns on his head and wings on his back. The implication is that things that are non-human, or natural, are evil and we should be frightened of them. By the 1800s, landscapes are generally either presented as Romantically grand and sublime, the work of an all-powerful deity, or tidied up and placed behind fences in the portraits of wealthy landowners. There are some exceptions to this movement, such as the engraver Thomas Bewick who created beautiful imagery of British wildlife while also putting scenes of rural deprivation into the background. Readers of his 1804 book, *History of British Birds,* would have been shocked to find images of a poverty-gripped beggar hanged from a tree alongside engravings of puffins, owls and sparrows. In fact, the othering of people from the countryside, those closer to Nature with their odd ways and customs, runs parallel with the othering of Nature itself. By the mid to late twentieth-century, villages and villagers were either portrayed as a source of ridicule or as a source of danger. Films such as 1966's The Witches send clear warnings about the kind of people who live in the countryside and what they get up to. Science fiction works such as *Village of the Damned,* based on John Wyndham's book *The Midwich Cuckoos*, show what dangers can grow in these remote, rural spaces. This movement finds its most potent expression through the genre of Folk Horror where evil seems to leach from the landscape, like it does from the dark corners of the animation of Watership Down.

And yet, there is a dichotomy here because it is the very things that Folk Horror tells us to fear that many fans of the genre have grown to love. Take, for example, probably the most famous Folk Horror film of them all, the 1972 film *The Wicker Man*. The moral of the film is crystal clear - be wary of people such as the residents of Summerisle with their connection to Nature and their old ways. It is a clear warning against paganism – and yet the film is warmly embraced by the pagan community, spawning several different cuts and even cult events such as the wonderful Sing-Along-A-Wicker-Man evenings. By ramping up the horror and terror of Nature and those most closely connected to it, directors and producers of Folk Horror made Nature wonderfully and gratifyingly terrifying. Rather than making us run away from it, they made a generation embrace the darkness, the mystery and the otherness of the natural world.

I do not like Nature being presented as homogenised and safe. If Nature were really like that it would, frankly, be quite boring. But there are limits to these things. The presentation of the natural world on television has changed in the last decade and seems insistent on presenting Nature as simply "red in tooth and claw." Even seemingly cosy programmes, such as BBC2's *Springwatch* can be a difficult watch at times, with audiences following somewhat anthropomorphised chicks in their nests, only to watch them be predated just before fledging. Ok, Nature is not nice and fluffy and safe. I know that but I do not want to see it every time I try to engage with a documentary on the natural world.

The point is that while *Watership Down* may have been a tough watch in 1978, it is not the same as watching an antelope being eaten alive while David Attenborough narrates every visceral detail. That approach reduces the value of Nature and strips it of its mystery. You see, dark as *Watership Down* may be, it is not just a film about threat, dislocation and loss. It is a film about hope and, more importantly, it is a beautifully spiritual film where the rabbits are deeply connected to the source, in this case, to Frith. It is that same connection to the Nature we see in the witches and cunning folk of the medieval period, in the engravings of Thomas Bewick and the good people of Summerisle. It is the same connection which I have been lucky enough to feel at times myself. But that connection to Nature is not always safe. It is awe inspiring and even terrifying. It is so much larger than I ever could have imagined. It hides in the forests and emanates from every living thing. It comes out of the soil and the hedgerows. It has been infusing our indigenous customs and beliefs for millennia. It is beyond any sense of reason and rationality that we have. It is quintessentially us and yet it is not at all human.

And that, I think, is the most wonderfully terrifying thing of all.

NIMUE BROWN

Beyond Inner Monologues

We're talking about desire, or at least, I am trying to have that conversation. *What do you want? What would make you happy?*

Peas, you tell me.

Not in words as such, but in an overwhelming sense of peas-ness that floods my mind. Green, lush, and numerous. Peas and more peas.

This surprises me. I hadn't expected a conversation at all, and I certainly hadn't expected this clear answer to my question. I digest it, unironically.

You, the people who dwell in my gut, are often unhappy. I'm not always sure why. I don't think I am a great environment – stress and a dodgy body structure probably make me less than ideal. But here we are, and you are in me and I am deeply affected by you and maybe if we talk, we can do better.

I take up chatting to you at

night. I ask for your cooperation on tough days when I really need my body to function.

Hello. people of the digestive system, can you work with me on this? Can we be allies? I'd like to be friends.

I bring you peas. Peas for appeasement, maybe. I bring you raw things, increasingly convinced that having vast amounts of plant matter agrees with you. The sourdough bread is acceptable and I wonder if you have a treaty now with the yeast people who live on my skin and in the air around me. Maybe that was the missing link all along, that I needed to set up communication between the people who live on my skin and the people who live inside me. Now if I could just persuade my womb and my adrenal glands not to attack you, we might make some progress.

I thought for a long time there was no reasoning with my womb. It has always been angry. However, a herbal remedy from a friend seems to placate it a little. Maybe it can be persuaded not to choose violence. It has never felt like mine, or part of me, I have no control over it, and it has been so full of rage for so long that I have come to think of it as an enemy. As for the adrenal glands, I get in to thank them for their return to action, even though that's been sporadic and unsettling. I think they are trying their best, and they've not had a good time of it over the years.

We're an uneasy alliance inside this skin. Not really a community but a gathering of pieces, entities, ideas and scars. We have been thrown together such that it would be better if we could figure out how to cooperate. I keep talking, hoping that it isn't a monologue, wanting to be a cooperative, not merely a crappy backdrop for the ecosystem inside me.

JACK WOLF

Afterword / Behemot

At first sight, it may seem that devoting this issue of Homecoming to 'Nature' is a bit of a cop-out: after all, from an animist perspective, the division between Human and Nature that is so characteristic of most modern ways of thinking is simply not there: Humans are a part of Nature, inescapably so, and Natural processes, therefore, are inextricably bound up with Human functioning at all levels, from the economic to the intestinal. But it is worth exploring this relationship – or set of relationships – more deeply, if only to avoid the opposite trap of taking 'Nature' for granted and so failing to understand or appreciate its importance, or see how this concept of relationality leads animist approaches to Nature to differ from those of other perspectives which, while superficially similar, emerge out of a very different set of ideas. As Jonathan Woolley discusses in his introduction to this issue, animist thinking runs contrary to that of the mainstream modernist project to the extent that even many environmentalists feel unable to admit its implications for fear of breaching a societal taboo around anthropomorphism. Animist positions towards the natural world are commonly misunderstood, being dismissed as sentimentalist or seen as a subset of New Age spirituality, when in fact animist thinking leans toward the practical rather than the sentimental, and focuses on the material and communal rather than on the spiritual and individual.

For instance, in this issue, Graham Harvey argues that it is, in his words: 'Sometimes ok for vegan animists to kill slugs'. That 'sometimes' is critical, of course – Harvey is not arguing for a wholesale slug massacre, or suggesting that in the case of the allotment harvest, the human need automatically takes precedence over that of the non-human; instead the argument hinges on the way relationships between species can sometimes become competitive. Slug killing, for Harvey, is acceptable because animism not a world view in which Nature is idealised: while humans are not inherently superior to slugs, allowing the slugs to run riot would would reinstate the division between human and natural that animist thinking tries to dissolve. Unlike romantic or pastoral traditions of thought, in which the non-human world acts as a separate – if often deeply loved – backdrop on which human concerns, both good and bad, can be projected, the animist relationship with Nature is by definition one in which the agency of both Nature and human as equal participants – (and yes, a slug can be said to have agency) – is paramount. Humans do not stand like wanderers above a sea of fog, surveying a wonderful natural world from a position far above it: instead, This, for Harvey, is practical reality as much as it is philosophy. Nature is beside us, and around us, and, importantly, within us.

Nimue Brown explores this bodily physicality and accords a degree of agency to the bacteria living in her own gut in 'Beyond Inner Monologues': 'What do you want?' she asks them. 'Peas,' they answer; and while 'Peas' is, indeed, what these little people seem to want, the homophone 'Peace' also immediately leaps to mind. Meanwhile, in her description of this year's Ceremony to celebrate the Autumn Equinox, Druid Cerri Lee offers a vision of how ritual can be used to honour and reinforce the deep connection between human and non-human beings, bringing body, mind and spirit into meaningful alignment: 'Without Peace,' she writes, 'no work can be'. While it may be fine for vegan animists to kill slugs (sometimes) it is long past time to end the nonsensical so-called war between the 'human' and the 'natural'. When the body of a human being can contain more bacterial cells than human ones, and these cells turn out to be necessary for the overall healthy functioning of the organism, where on Earth is the dividing line between the one being and the other?

None of this is to suggest, of course, that the natural world (humans, slugs, and bacteria all included) is entirely peaceable. While musing on what it was like to grow up in a world in which connectivity between the human and natural worlds was denied, in his discussion of the 'terror' that often inheres in modern depictions of the natural world Andrew Anderson ponders whether a 1970s childhood experience of being taken to see Watership Down heightened his developing awareness of the uncanny within the natural; he concludes that Nature has her own terrors, which actually constitute a large part of what drew him towards animist relationship in the first place. In her memoir, Rachel Bentham describes another 70s childhood, in which the experience of raising – and losing – several orphaned starlings allows a lonely child to forge an affectionate relationship with a non-human being that offers an emotional outlet and a wider perspective on the world, despite a cultural context in which the distinction between 'us' and 'them' is strongly policed. But the title 'Migrants' reminds us throughout of another kind of othering – the one that divides one group of human beings from another. As Woolley points out in his introduction: 'if you can't see personhood in everyone, then it can potentially be stripped from anyone.'

Homecoming

The impulse toward entering into relationship with nature often begins with an appreciation for the natural world that has a lot in common with romanticism, or with environmentalist concerns for the fate of non-human beings in a world ruthlessly dominated by the human species. Nancy M Bell encapsulates a sense of this initial connection in her pair of poems 'February Breath' and 'November Ice', while Kate Hawkey describes how an encounter with a tree in her local city park allows her respite from the 'anxiety of a future arriving too soon.' Frank Olding, in 'Cadno / Fox' – incidentally also the first Welsh language poem to be published in *Homecoming* with a free verse English translation – speaks of the impact of generations of human persecution on the behaviour of one wild individual in a humanised landscape of walls and 'bitter upland[s]'. Gordon MacLellan points out in 'London Plane Tree' that no-one has ever told the city trees that they are not free: the wild remains present in all things and all places, regardless of the impact of urban sprawl and wholly ignorant of a human concern that maintains a degree of separation in order to generate what MacLellan calls the 'whole "nature connection" industry'. Jon Nash, in 'Back to Nature', writes from the perspective of an individual living within modernity of his desire for a psychological connection with nature that goes far beyond the pastoral – to become a tree, rather than hug one. Helen Smith picks up this same idea in two different ways in 'naked, animal' and in 'reincarnation' – written from the point of view of a spider remembering a previous human lifetime in which she trod upon a spider – suggesting that such deep connection is not only desirable, but inevitable. Hannah Willow, who is also this issue's cover artist, erases distinctions between within and without herself as an experience of lying under a night sky brings about a feeling of homecoming to both place and to her own body: "my bones" she writes, "are the dust of my ancestors / and grass grows under my skin". In a similar vein, in 'The day the moss first started to grow' Miranda L Barnes describes an experience of becoming forest: while we do not know whether the 'you' of the poem is human or not, or alive or not, it does not matter – such exclusive categories are revealed to be meaningless when we are wholly immersed within the more-than-human world. On the other hand, in 'Auguries' she describes how an apparently surface level connection between human and non-human beings – watching the birds – can reveal deeper patterns at work below the skin and hint at future possibilities. That sense of the 'uncanny' existing within the natural world that Anderson encountered as a child is at work here, too, revealed in the choreography of the pigeons and the deaths of baby chicks.

The animist thinker David Abrams, describing being awake to the beauty in animist reality as a strategy to cope with dark times, describes the fricative 'j' at the start of the word 'joy' as an incidence of the "shadow that is laced through the real world: danger, loss, illness; all this difficult stuff that creates the friction that makes something joyful, rather than just happy'*. Perhaps what the shadow movements of the birds and the uneasy feeling provoked in one small boy by a display of teasels on a window-sill ultimately portend is that, as a species, we will be forced to break out of a delusional regime of thinking that has brought us to a point where re-establishing relationship with nature has become a survival imperative. But what that shadow also reminds us, because it must, is that after several hundred years of reinforcement and with vested interests and societal norms intent on perpetuating the status quo, this change will not be without friction.

Back in the 1820s, the essayist Leigh Hunt, unnerved by the changes then being wrought by humankind on the non-human world by encroaching industrialisation, wrote to a friend: 'I hope you paid your devotions as usual to the old religion and hung up an evergreen. If you all go on so there will be a hope someday that a voice will be heard along the water saying 'the great God Pan is alive again!' upon which the villagers will leave off starving and singing profane hymns and fall to dancing again.' Hunt's vision, though somewhat flippantly expressed and grounded in romanticised classical imagery rather than animist thinking, nevertheless expresses a desire for a world in which the human and the non-human are so far from being in conflict that previously starving villagers have time and energy to be able to dance. Unfortunately, he was writing at the end-of-the-beginning of what has since become the most destructive techno-complex phase in human history, and would never see the philosophy he espoused make any significant impact. We, however, are standing at what, most probably, is the beginning of the end. And unlike Hunt, we know that far from being wanderers above the sea of fog, we are swimmers deeply immersed within it. So we have to hope – and for our own human sakes, as much as for the other-than-humans who share our reality, we have to try.

Wanderer above the Sea of Fog by German Romanticist artist Caspar David Friedrich, 1818.

* in conversation, Animate Earth Confluence, Nov 2024.

Behemot

We walk – the boy and I – up to King Arthur's Hall
Over Ladydown from Penvorder in the mist.
The footpath takes us through the scattered gorse,
Sheep-haunted yellow flowers, shivering
On over enclosed fields, onto the cattle land.

They are hardy breeds: Highlands and Belted Galloways,
Long horned, tough coated, modern Aurochs
Staring off into the distance, stamping bullish feet,
Imprinting letter Bs into the smooth earth, breathing
clouds.
And we – the boy and I – we walk

Maintaining a respectful space between ourselves
And these, a space that whispers
Behemot – the Hebrew word for creatures:
Bet hey mem vav tau, five letters brought to life
By vagrant breath, *ruach* sown through sky.

They turn their heads, heavy as boulders, as we walk
Watching us, through damp light, as we walk
Across a mat of sheep's fescue, heath's bedstraw,
common bent,
Up to the foresters' stockade, up to
King Arthur's Hall, the place of sanctuary.

Six hundred years ago, they say – that is,
Five clear-cut centuries before the trees came down
To feed the smelting furnaces and power the beams,
This mist-lit marsh was thronged with *behemot*:
Brown bear, wild boar, elk, lynx.

Homecoming

So then the cow-herds commandeered
This rectangle of ancient stones, this mortuary ground,
And built on it a pound to muster strays, complete with ten-foot palisade
Of wood and daub, thrown up on steep stone banks;
Set fire to frighten the night-wolves,

The wanderers. Now, just the half-tamed cattle are kept out:
Un-grazed, the heather sprouts bright crimson from the banks.
White cottongrass quickens the bog beneath.
We stay – the boy and I – we stay
Just long enough to hear the silence breathing.

*

King Arthur's Hall is on Bodmin Moor. Previously thought to be mediaeval, recent research has revealed it to be of Neolithic origin.

List of Contributors

Jonathan Woolley is a druid, diviner and an environmental anthropologist, whose research deals with how myth, culture and ritual shape our relationship with the natural world. Jonathan has written extensively on traditional customs, enchantment, and the landscape for numerous academic publications; including *Implicit Religion*, the *Kings Review, Environmental Humanities*, and *Anthropology Today,* and is a regular contributor for *Cunning Folk,* an independent magazine covering magic, mythology, folklore and the occult. Jonathan recently co-edited *Modern Religious Druidry: Studies in Paganism, Celtic Identity, and Nature Spirituality,* the first collation of academic research into the beliefs and customs of contemporary Druids. As part of his Druidic practice, Jonathan regularly tells fortunes, through scrying, tarot, and the reading of omens in the land, sea and sky. As a member of the Order of Bards, Ovates, and Druids since 2010, Jonathan has played an active role in leading and supporting seasonal rituals and advocacy for the Pagan Community.

Miranda Lynn Barnes is a poet from the US living near Nottingham, England. Her debut pamphlet, *Blue Dot Aubade*, was published with V. Press in 2020. *Formulations*, a chapbook of new poetic forms based in chemistry, was co-written with Stephen Paul Wren and published in March 2022 (Small Press/Tangent Books). Her poem "In the Pines" was awarded second place in the Verve Poetry Competition 2023, judged by Forward Prize winner Kim Moore. Miranda's poems have appeared in *Poetry Wales, Under the Radar, EcoTheo Review, Shearsman, Tears in the Fence,* and other journals and anthologies, both in the UK and abroad. Find out more at **https://mirandalynnbarnes.wordpress.com/**

Rachel Bentham teaches Creative Writing at the Universities of Bristol and Oxford. She's hoping to settle into a comfortable retirement doing what she loves; writing and making textiles. Much published and broadcast, currently working on a poetry collection focused on trees, titled *Heartwood.*

Nancy M Bell lives in Castor, Alberta. She is a member of the Writers Guild of Alberta, and the Canadian Authors Association. Her poem Birds was nominated for the PushCart Awards. **http://www.nancymbell.ca**

Helen Smith is a neurodivergent creative living on the north-east coast of Scotland. With a background in zoology and psychology, she is inspired by mythology, relationships between people and nature, and the landscape of the body. Although she prefers woodlands over the internet, she can be found at **helensmithwrites.com.**

Kate Hawkey has worked in history education at the University of Bristol for many years. She has written about history, environmental crises, and the need for curriculum change. These concerns continue to inform her work although in recent years she has moved from academic writing towards more creative short forms.

Gordon MacLellan is a writer, poet and storyteller whose work explores the relationships between people, places, passion and wildlife. As Creeping Toad, he works with community groups to find ways of celebrating those relationships. Other writings include *Old Stones and Ancient Bones* (poems, direct from Gordon) and *Sacred Animals* (Green Magic Books, 2023) Find out more: **creepingtoad.blogspot.com** Social media**: creeping toad**

Graham Harvey is emeritus professor of religious studies at The Open University, UK. He has researched with Jews,

Pagans and Indigenous peoples. Most of his recent work has engaged with "the new animism". He lives in Northumberland and has recently taken on an allotment in an effort to discover what "retirement" means.

Theresa Kelleher is a poet and traditional storyteller. Most of her work recognises the kinship and deep connection with all beings. She is currently working on her poetry collection Mystical Tenderness.

Frank Olding lives in Abergavenny. He is a retired archaeologist, a poet and a pagan druid. He writes in Welsh and has published two collections. He is a member of the Gorsedd of Bards and a Fellow of the Society of Antiquaries. He recently published *The Taliesin Sourcebook* (Green Magic).

Jon Nash is a poet, playwright, and theatre director based in Devon, England. His work explores truth in the digital age, our relationship with the wild during the climate crisis and animism. You can find him at **jonnash.uk** and on Instagram at **@jonnashwriter**

Cerri Lee is a Druid, Gardener, Artist, Writer, living in Sussex between the rolling chalk hills and the seashore. Cerri is an Animist to her core, alongside the inspiration found in myth and folklore, it is the foundation to every ritual she writes, her art and philosophy of life.

Andrew Anderson is the current editor of OBOD's magazine, Touchstone. He has written three books, all published by Moon Books; *The Ritual of Writing, Artio and Artaois,* and *The Magic of Cats*. His book on Herne the Hunter is forthcoming.

Nimue Brown is the author of assorted Pagan and Druid titles, published by Moon Books and also self-published. She lives on the Cotswold edge above the Severn River, and talks to everything. She is a longstanding blogger at **www.druidlife.wordpress.com.**

Jack Wolf' set up AUP in 2022 in response to the urgent need to rethink western relastionships with the more than human world. Their first novel *The Tale of Raw Head and Bloody Bones* (Chatto and Windus) was published in 2013 and their second novel, *Mammoth and Crow*, by AUP in 2022. Visit: **aurochspress.co.uk**

*

Hannah Willow is an artist and writer based in North Cornwall. Inspired by folklore, mythology and the stories held within the land, she works in paint, pencil and silver. Her writing is her connection to the land and the stories held within that inform all of my work.
www.HannahWillow.com.

Carrie Osborne has a lifelong love of drawing focusing particularly on themes of nature, mythology and the human figure. She explores her responses to the natural world through both images and prose poetry, using mainly pen & ink, watercolour and more recently relief printmaking.

*

Note

Where contributors are based in the US, Canada, or other countries where US spelling and punctuation rules are commonly used, these have been retained in accordance with the localist ethos of animist practise.

Homecoming

www.ingramcontent.com/pod-product-compliance
Lightning Source LLC
Chambersburg PA
CBHW061223210726
48294CB00006B/1966

* 9 7 8 1 7 3 9 6 9 7 2 7 3 *